About Skill Builders

Fractions, D[e]cimals, and Percents

Grades 3–5

Welcome to Skill Builders *Fractions, Decimals, and Percents* for grades 3–5. This book uses focused practice to reinforce the connections between these math concepts. This full-color workbook contains grade-level-appropriate activities based on national standards to help ensure that children master basic skills before progressing.

More than 70 pages of activities cover essential skills, including simplifying and renaming fractions, adding and subtracting fractions, multiplying fractions, and converting fractions, decimals, and percentages. The book's colorful, inviting format, easy-to-follow directions, and clear examples help build children's confidence and make fractions, decimals, and percentages more accessible and enjoyable.

The Skill Builders series offers workbooks that are perfect for keeping children current during the school year or preparing them for the next grade.

www.carsondellosa.com
Carson-Dellosa Publishing LLC
Greensboro, North Carolina

Printed in the USA • All rights reserved.

ISBN 978-1-936023-17-2
09-134181151

Table of Contents

Identifying Fractions

A fraction is a value written so the bottom number, called the **denominator**, tells you how many equal parts make up the whole. The top number—the **numerator**—tells how many parts you have.

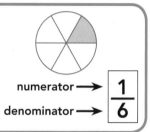

numerator ⟶ $\dfrac{1}{6}$ ⟵ denominator

Write the correct fraction.

1.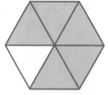

2.

3.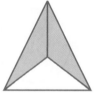

4.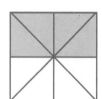

5.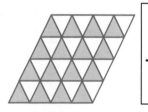

6.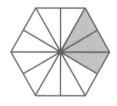

A Fraction Is Part of a Whole

$\frac{3}{4}$ of the circle is shaded. $\frac{1}{4}$ of the circle is not shaded.

$\frac{3}{4}$ ← part shaded   **numerator**   part not shaded → $\frac{1}{4}$
← total parts   **denominator**   total parts →

On the first line, write the fraction for the part that is shaded. On the second line, write the fraction for the part that is not shaded.

1. 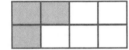   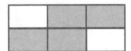   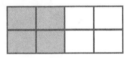

    ___   ___   ___
    ___   ___   ___

2.

    ___   ___   ___
    ___   ___   ___

3.

    ___   ___   ___
    ___   ___   ___

4.       

    ___   ___   ___
    ___   ___   ___

A Fraction Is Part of a Whole

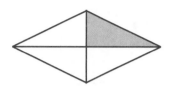

$\frac{1}{4}$ of the rhombus is shaded. | $\frac{4}{8}$ or $\frac{1}{2}$ of the circle is shaded.

Shade in the following fractions.

1. $\frac{1}{2}$ $\frac{3}{4}$

2. $\frac{3}{4}$  $\frac{1}{4}$

3. $\frac{7}{8}$  $\frac{2}{8}$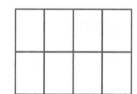

4. $\frac{2}{3}$ $\frac{1}{3}$

5. $\frac{5}{8}$ $\frac{2}{8}$

A Fraction Is Part of a Whole

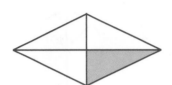

$\frac{1}{4}$ of the rhombus is shaded. | $\frac{2}{3}$ of the circle is not shaded.

$\frac{1}{4}$ is read as **one-fourth**. | $\frac{2}{3}$ is read as **two-thirds**.

Write the following words as fractions.

1. three-fifths _____

2. four-ninths _____

3. one-third _____

4. two-eighths _____

5. four-fifths _____

6. one-half _____

Write the words for each of the given fractions.

7. $\frac{1}{3}$ _____

8. $\frac{1}{2}$ _____

9. $\frac{3}{8}$ _____

10. $\frac{2}{5}$ _____

Comparing Fractions

The more parts the whole is divided into, the smaller the fraction is. Or, the larger the denominator, the smaller the fraction.

Use the fraction table to help you think about which fraction is greater. Use >, <, or = to compare the fractions.

1. $\frac{1}{2} \bigcirc \frac{1}{4}$

2. $\frac{2}{3} \bigcirc \frac{1}{3}$

3. $\frac{1}{4} \bigcirc \frac{1}{6}$

4. $\frac{4}{8} \bigcirc \frac{4}{10}$

5. $\frac{1}{12} \bigcirc \frac{1}{10}$

6. $\frac{3}{4} \bigcirc \frac{3}{8}$

7. $\frac{3}{8} \bigcirc \frac{10}{12}$

8. $\frac{2}{8} \bigcirc \frac{7}{8}$

9. $\frac{1}{5} \bigcirc \frac{1}{4}$

10. $\frac{1}{6} \bigcirc \frac{1}{3}$

11. $\frac{3}{12} \bigcirc \frac{1}{3}$

12. $\frac{1}{2} \bigcirc \frac{1}{1}$

Naming Fractions Equal To and Greater Than One

This fraction shows $\frac{5}{3}$. $\frac{5}{3}$ is called an **improper fraction** because the numerator is larger than the denominator. $\frac{3}{3}$ equals one whole, so $\frac{5}{3}$ equals 1 whole plus $\frac{2}{3}$. $1\frac{2}{3}$ is called a **mixed number**.

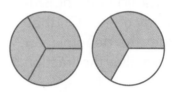

$\frac{5}{3}$ or $1\frac{2}{3}$

Write each fraction as an improper fraction and then as a mixed number.

1.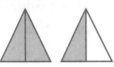

_____ or _____

2.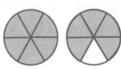

_____ or _____

3.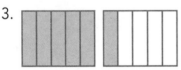

_____ or _____

4.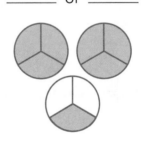

_____ or _____

5.

_____ or _____

6.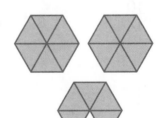

_____ or _____

Rewriting Fractions as Mixed Numbers

$\frac{14}{3}$ is an improper fraction.

$\frac{14}{3}$ can be rewritten as

$14 \div 3$ or $3\overline{)14}$.

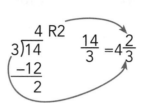

$$\begin{array}{r} 4 \text{ R2} \\ 3\overline{)14} \\ -12 \\ \hline 2 \end{array}$$

$\frac{14}{3} = 4\frac{2}{3}$

2 becomes the numerator; the denominator stays as 3.

$4\frac{2}{3}$ is a mixed number.

Rewrite each fraction as a mixed number.

1. $\frac{5}{4} =$

2. $\frac{10}{3} =$

3. $\frac{9}{8} =$

4. $\frac{5}{2} =$

5. $\frac{7}{4} =$

6. $\frac{9}{3} =$

7. $\frac{10}{7} =$

8. $\frac{19}{8} =$

9. $\frac{9}{5} =$

10. $\frac{23}{10} =$

11. $\frac{17}{8} =$

12. $\frac{13}{3} =$

13. $\frac{28}{9} =$

14. $\frac{9}{4} =$

15. $\frac{13}{6} =$

Rewriting Fractions as Mixed Numbers

Rewrite each fraction as a mixed number.

1. $\frac{15}{2}$ =

2. $\frac{7}{4}$ =

3. $\frac{20}{7}$ =

4. $\frac{43}{5}$ =

5. $\frac{23}{8}$ =

6. $\frac{21}{5}$ =

7. $\frac{31}{12}$ =

8. $\frac{5}{2}$ =

9. $\frac{13}{8}$ =

10. $\frac{11}{4}$ =

11. $\frac{49}{9}$ =

12. $\frac{41}{6}$ =

Changing Mixed Numbers to Improper Fractions

$$3\frac{1}{3} = \frac{(3 \times 3) + 1}{3}$$

$$= \frac{9 + 1}{3}$$

$$= \frac{10}{3}$$

To change mixed numbers to improper fractions:
1. Multiply the whole number by the denominator
2. Add the numerator.
3. The denominator remains the same.

Rewrite each mixed number as an improper fraction.

1. $2\frac{1}{3} =$

2. $6\frac{3}{4} =$

3. $1\frac{1}{12} =$

4. $3\frac{1}{8} =$

5. $7\frac{3}{5} =$

6. $1\frac{9}{10} =$

7. $3\frac{2}{5} =$

8. $9\frac{4}{11} =$

9. $3\frac{6}{7} =$

10. $5\frac{4}{5} =$

11. $4\frac{5}{12} =$

12. $6\frac{7}{11} =$

Simplifying Fractions

$\frac{4}{8} = \frac{4 \div 4}{8 \div 4}$

$= \frac{1}{2}$

A fraction is **simplified** when 1 is the only number that divides into both the numerator and the denominator.

To simplify, you divide the numerator and denominator by the same number.

Simplify each fraction.

1. $\frac{2}{8} =$

2. $\frac{6}{15} =$

3. $\frac{8}{24} =$

4. $\frac{4}{6} =$

5. $\frac{5}{15} =$

6. $\frac{6}{10} =$

7. $\frac{6}{8} =$

8. $\frac{2}{24} =$

9. $\frac{8}{12} =$

10. $\frac{3}{9} =$

11. $\frac{6}{24} =$

12. $\frac{10}{12} =$

Simplifying Mixed Numbers

$2\frac{15}{20} = 2 + \frac{15}{20}$

$\phantom{2\frac{15}{20}} = 2 + \frac{3}{4}$

$\phantom{2\frac{15}{20}} = \mathbf{2\frac{3}{4}}$

When simplifying mixed numbers, simplify the fraction.

Simplify each mixed number.

1. $2\frac{2}{4} =$

2. $3\frac{5}{15} =$

3. $2\frac{12}{16} =$

4. $1\frac{6}{9} =$

5. $6\frac{4}{8} =$

6. $6\frac{3}{3} =$

7. $2\frac{5}{20} =$

8. $4\frac{7}{21} =$

9. $1\frac{3}{6} =$

10. $4\frac{3}{9} =$

11. $5\frac{3}{12} =$

12. $2\frac{3}{12} =$

Simplest Form

Simplify each fraction.

1. $\dfrac{6}{18} =$

2. $\dfrac{12}{18} =$

3. $\dfrac{20}{24} =$

4. $\dfrac{18}{24} =$

5. $\dfrac{9}{54} =$

6. $\dfrac{6}{12} =$

Write each fraction as a mixed number in simplest form.

7. $\dfrac{9}{8} =$

8. $\dfrac{11}{5} =$

9. $\dfrac{16}{6} =$

10. $\dfrac{16}{3} =$

11. $\dfrac{24}{16} =$

12. $\dfrac{18}{4} =$

13. $1\dfrac{5}{15} =$

14. $2\dfrac{4}{6} =$

15. $4\dfrac{3}{12} =$

Renaming Fractions

 To **rename** a fraction, multiply the numerator and denominator by the same number.

$\frac{1}{3}$ of the circle is shaded.

$\frac{1}{3} = \frac{1}{3} \times \frac{2}{2} = \frac{2}{6}$

$\frac{2}{6}$ of the circle is shaded.

$\frac{4}{5} \rightarrow \frac{}{10}$

Think: To get from 5 to 10, multiply by 2.

So, $\frac{4}{5} = \frac{4}{5} \times \frac{2}{2} = \frac{8}{10}$

$\frac{2}{3} \rightarrow \frac{}{12}$

Think: To get from 3 to 12, multiply by 4.

So, $\frac{2}{3} = \frac{2}{3} \times \frac{4}{4} = \frac{8}{12}$

Rename the following fractions using the denominator given.

1. $\frac{3}{4} = \frac{}{12}$

2. $\frac{4}{5} = \frac{}{15}$

3. $\frac{2}{3} = \frac{}{6}$

4. $\frac{1}{4} = \frac{}{16}$

5. $\frac{5}{6} = \frac{}{18}$

6. $\frac{3}{5} = \frac{}{20}$

7. $\frac{5}{8} = \frac{}{24}$

8. $\frac{2}{7} = \frac{}{14}$

9. $\frac{5}{6} = \frac{}{12}$

Finding Equivalent Fractions

Equivalent fractions are fractions that are equal to each other. To find equivalent fractions, multiply the numerator and the denominator by the same number.

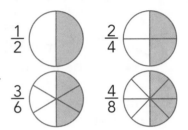

$$\frac{1}{2} \times \frac{2}{2} = \frac{2}{4} \qquad \frac{1}{2} \times \frac{3}{3} = \frac{3}{6} \qquad \frac{1}{2} \times \frac{4}{4} = \frac{4}{8}$$

Cross out the fraction that is not equivalent to the first fraction.

1. $\frac{1}{3} =$ $\frac{2}{6}$ $\frac{3}{9}$ $\frac{4}{8}$ $\frac{5}{15}$

2. $\frac{1}{4} =$ $\frac{2}{8}$ $\frac{3}{6}$ $\frac{4}{16}$ $\frac{5}{20}$

3. $\frac{1}{5} =$ $\frac{2}{6}$ $\frac{2}{10}$ $\frac{3}{15}$ $\frac{4}{20}$

4. $\frac{2}{3} =$ $\frac{4}{6}$ $\frac{6}{9}$ $\frac{8}{16}$ $\frac{10}{15}$

Fill in the missing number.

5. $\frac{1}{4} = \frac{3}{}$

6. $\frac{2}{} = \frac{4}{6}$

7. $\frac{5}{8} = \frac{}{16}$

8. $\frac{3}{4} = \frac{9}{}$

9. $\frac{}{6} = \frac{2}{12}$

10. $\frac{2}{3} = \frac{}{9}$

Greatest Common Factor

A **factor** is a number that another number can be divided by evenly.

Example:

List the factors of 12 and 18.
Factors of 12: 1, 2, 3, 4, 6, 12   Factors of 18: 1, 2, 3, 6, 9, 18

Circle the common factors.
Factors of 12: (1)(2)(3) 4,(6) 12   Factors of 18: (1)(2)(3)(6) 9, 18

Write the greatest common factor (GCF).
GCF: 6

List the factors of each pair of numbers. Circle the common factors. Find the greatest common factor (GCF).

1. 6:
   18:
   GCF:_____

2. 4:
   12:
   GCF:_____

3. 12:
   18:
   GCF:_____

4. 14:
   21:
   GCF:_____

5. 18:
   27:
   GCF:_____

6. 24:
   32:
   GCF:_____

7. 9:
   12:
   GCF:_____

8. 9:
   15:
   GCF:____

Simplest Form

Example:

Write the fraction $\frac{42}{56}$ in simplest form.

Step 1
Find the GCF of the
numerator and denominator.
42: ①,②,3, 6,⑦,⑭ 21, 42
56: ①,②,4,⑦,8, ⑭ 28, 56
GCF: 14

Step 2
Divide the numerator
and denominator by
their GCF.

$$\frac{42}{56} \div \frac{14}{14} = \frac{3}{4}$$

Write each fraction in simplest form. Circle your answer. If a fraction is already in simplest form, just write the fraction.

1. $\frac{4}{6}$

2. $\frac{5}{10}$

3. $\frac{9}{15}$

4. $\frac{3}{27}$

5. $\frac{5}{18}$

6. $\frac{15}{18}$

7. $\frac{6}{21}$

8. $\frac{28}{42}$

9. $\frac{22}{30}$

10. $\frac{7}{21}$

11 $\frac{19}{38}$

12. $\frac{48}{60}$

13. $\frac{34}{59}$

14. $\frac{22}{88}$

15. $\frac{26}{28}$

Least Common Multiple

The **least common multiple (LCM)** is the smallest number that is a multiple of two or more numbers.

Example:

Find the LCM of 6 and 8.

1. List some multiples of 6 and 8.
2. Circle the common multiples.
3. Write the least common multiple.

Multiples of 6:
6, 12, 18, ⟨24⟩, 30, 36, 42, ⟨48⟩

Multiples of 8:
8, 16, ⟨24⟩, 32, 40, ⟨48⟩

LCM = **24**

Find the least common multiple (LCM) of each pair of numbers.

1. 6:
   2:
   LCM: _____

2. 4:
   8:
   LCM: _____

3. 5:
   3:
   LCM: _____

4. 4:
   6:
   LCM: _____

5. 8:
   12:
   LCM: _____

6. 6:
   10:
   LCM: _____

7. 12:
   20:
   LCM: _____

8. 10:
   15:
   LCM: _____

9. 8:
   10:
   LCM: _____

10. 4:
    18:
    LCM: _____

Lowest Common Denominator

Two fractions have a common denominator if their denominators are the same. **The lowest common denominator (LCD)** of two fractions is the least common multiple of their denominators.

Step 1
Find the LCD of the two fractions.

$$\frac{5}{8} \text{ and } \frac{7}{12}$$

8: 8, 16, (24)
12: 12, (24)

LCD: 24

Step 2
Write equivalent fractions with the common denominator of 24.

$$\frac{5}{8} = \frac{}{24}$$

$$\frac{5}{8} = \frac{5}{8} \times \frac{3}{3} = \frac{15}{24}$$

$$\frac{7}{12} = \frac{}{24}$$

$$\frac{7}{12} = \frac{7}{12} \times \frac{2}{2} = \frac{14}{24}$$

Write two equivalent fractions using the LCD.

1. $\frac{1}{9}$ and $\frac{1}{3}$ _____ _____

2. $\frac{1}{3}$ and $\frac{1}{6}$ _____ _____

3. $\frac{4}{8}$ and $\frac{2}{3}$ _____ _____

4. $\frac{2}{6}$ and $\frac{3}{9}$ _____ _____

5. $\frac{2}{4}$ and $\frac{3}{7}$ _____ _____

6. $\frac{2}{3}$ and $\frac{6}{8}$ _____ _____

7. $\frac{1}{8}$ and $\frac{1}{16}$ _____ _____

8. $\frac{1}{12}$ and $\frac{1}{4}$ _____ _____

9. $\frac{6}{9}$ and $\frac{3}{18}$ _____ _____

10. $\frac{2}{8}$ and $\frac{4}{32}$ _____ _____

Comparing and Ordering Fractions

To compare fractions, you need common denominators.

Example:

Compare $\frac{5}{7} = \frac{7}{9}$.

Step 1
Find the LCD.

7, 7, 14, 21, 28, 35, 42, 49, 56, ⑥③

9: 9, 18, 27, 36, 45, 54, ⑥③

LCD: 63

Step 2
Write equivalent fractions with the LCD.

$\frac{5}{7} = \frac{}{63}$

$\frac{5}{7} = \frac{5}{7} \times \frac{9}{9} = \frac{45}{63}$

$\frac{7}{9} = \frac{}{24}$

$\frac{7}{9} = \frac{7}{9} \times \frac{7}{7} = \frac{49}{33}$

Step 3
Compare the numerators.

$\frac{45}{63} < \frac{49}{63}$

Compare. Write >, <, or = in the ◯ in each problem.

1. $\frac{3}{6}$ ◯ $\frac{4}{8}$

2. $\frac{4}{5}$ ◯ $\frac{10}{15}$

3. $\frac{3}{5}$ ◯ $\frac{1}{2}$

4. $\frac{2}{3}$ ◯ $\frac{5}{8}$

5. $\frac{1}{3}$ ◯ $\frac{2}{5}$

6. $\frac{1}{8}$ ◯ $\frac{1}{16}$

7. $\frac{3}{5}$ ◯ $\frac{2}{3}$

8. $\frac{7}{10}$ ◯ $\frac{2}{3}$

9. $\frac{5}{8}$ ◯ $\frac{10}{16}$

Order from least to greatest.

10. $\frac{1}{3}, \frac{7}{12}, \frac{5}{6}$

11. $\frac{3}{4}, \frac{7}{8}, \frac{13}{16}$

12. $\frac{5}{6}, \frac{3}{4}, \frac{1}{2}$

13. $\frac{3}{7}, \frac{3}{5}, \frac{3}{8}$

Problem Solving

Math Balls

2½ cups peanut butter   5⅝ cups coconut

1⅞ cups honey   ⅝ cups raisins

two and one-half
teaspoons vanilla

You want to make Math Balls, but you only have 3 measuring cups in the following sizes: 1-cup, ¼-cup, and ⅓-cup. Use the recipe above to solve the following problems.

1. You measure 2 cups of peanut butter into the mixing bowl. How many ¼ cups will you need to complete the recipe?

2. Will you use your ¼ cup or ⅓ cup to measure the honey?

3. Write the mixed number for the amount of vanilla you will need to add.

4. How many cups of coconut will you need to add? (Do not include an improper fraction.)

5. How many cups of raisins will you need? (Do not include an improper fraction.)

6. What ingredient do you add the most of?

Adding Fractions

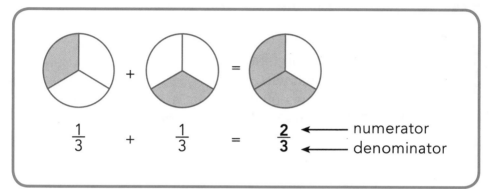

$\frac{1}{3}$ + $\frac{1}{3}$ = $\frac{2}{3}$ ← numerator
  ← denominator

Fill in the blanks, and shade in the blank objects using the information given.

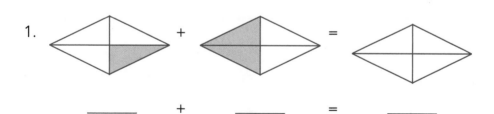

$\frac{1}{2}$ + $\frac{1}{2}$ = $\frac{2}{2}$ or 1

1.

_____ + _____ = _____

2.

_____ + _____ = _____

Adding Fractions
with Like Denominators

When adding fractions with like denominators:
1. Add the numerators.
2. Keep the same denominator.
3. Simplify if possible.

$$\begin{array}{r} \frac{2}{5} \\ +\ \frac{1}{5} \\ \hline \frac{3}{5} \end{array}$$

$$\begin{array}{r} \frac{5}{12} \\ +\ \frac{5}{12} \\ \hline \frac{10}{12} = \frac{5}{6} \end{array}$$

Add. Simplify if possible.

1. $\begin{array}{r} \frac{3}{5} \\ +\ \frac{1}{5} \\ \hline \end{array}$

2. $\begin{array}{r} \frac{1}{3} \\ +\ \frac{1}{3} \\ \hline \end{array}$

3. $\begin{array}{r} \frac{1}{6} \\ +\ \frac{3}{6} \\ \hline \end{array}$

4. $\begin{array}{r} \frac{1}{7} \\ +\ \frac{2}{7} \\ \hline \end{array}$

5. $\begin{array}{r} \frac{1}{4} \\ +\ \frac{1}{4} \\ \hline \end{array}$

6. $\begin{array}{r} \frac{1}{12} \\ +\ \frac{4}{12} \\ \hline \end{array}$

7. $\begin{array}{r} \frac{3}{6} \\ +\ \frac{2}{6} \\ \hline \end{array}$

8. $\begin{array}{r} \frac{1}{11} \\ +\ \frac{3}{11} \\ \hline \end{array}$

9. $\begin{array}{r} \frac{3}{8} \\ +\ \frac{3}{8} \\ \hline \end{array}$

10. $\begin{array}{r} \frac{2}{9} \\ +\ \frac{2}{9} \\ \hline \end{array}$

11. $\begin{array}{r} \frac{3}{12} \\ +\ \frac{5}{12} \\ \hline \end{array}$

12. $\begin{array}{r} \frac{5}{11} \\ +\ \frac{2}{11} \\ \hline \end{array}$

Adding Mixed Numbers with Like Denominators

$3\frac{2}{6}$

$+\ 2\frac{1}{6}$

$5\frac{3}{6}$

$=\ 5\frac{1}{2}$

1. Add the fractions.
2. Add the whole numbers.
3. Simplify if possible.

$2\frac{5}{12}$

$+\ 1\frac{11}{12}$

$3\frac{16}{12} = 3 + 1 + \frac{4}{12}$

$= 4\frac{1}{3}$

Add. Simplify if possible.

1. $3\frac{1}{3}$

    $+\ 2\frac{1}{3}$

2. $4\frac{2}{5}$

    $+\ \frac{1}{5}$

3. $3\frac{3}{8}$

    $+\ 2\frac{5}{8}$

4. $2\frac{4}{5}$

    $+\ 3\frac{2}{5}$

5. $13\frac{5}{8}$

    $+\ \frac{7}{8}$

6. $1\frac{3}{4}$

    $+\ 2\frac{3}{4}$

7. $10\frac{2}{9}$

    $+\ 2\frac{7}{9}$

8. $3\frac{5}{6}$

    $+\ 2\frac{3}{6}$

9. $2\frac{7}{10}$

    $+\ 1\frac{4}{10}$

10. $5\frac{4}{8}$

    $+\ \frac{2}{8}$

11. $3\frac{7}{12}$

    $+\ 4\frac{9}{12}$

12. $8\frac{7}{9}$

    $+\ 9\frac{5}{9}$

Adding Fractions with Unlike Denominators

When adding fractions with unlike denominators:

1. Find the least common denominator (LCD).
2. Rewrite each fraction using the LCD.
3. Add.
4. Simplify if possible.

$$\frac{5}{6} \longrightarrow \frac{5}{6} \times \frac{5}{5} \longrightarrow \frac{25}{30}$$

$$+ \frac{2}{5} \longrightarrow \frac{2}{5} \times \frac{6}{6} \longrightarrow \frac{12}{30}$$

$$\frac{37}{30}$$

$$= 1\frac{7}{30}$$

Add. Simplify if possible.

1. $\frac{2}{5}$
    $+ \frac{1}{3}$

2. $\frac{3}{8}$
    $+ \frac{1}{3}$

3. $\frac{1}{2}$
    $+ \frac{1}{3}$

4. $\frac{5}{6}$
    $+ \frac{2}{5}$

5. $\frac{2}{7}$
    $+ \frac{2}{3}$

6. $\frac{3}{10}$
    $+ \frac{1}{3}$

7. $\frac{3}{4}$
    $+ \frac{1}{7}$

8. $\frac{1}{3}$
    $+ \frac{5}{8}$

9. $\frac{1}{3}$
    $+ \frac{3}{4}$

Adding Mixed Numbers with Unlike Denominators

When adding mixed numbers with unlike denominators:

1. Find the least common denominator (LCD).
2. Rewrite each fraction using the LCD.
3. Add the whole numbers; then add the fractions.
4. Simplify if possible.

$$2\frac{1}{3} \longrightarrow \frac{1}{3} \times \frac{4}{4} \longrightarrow \frac{4}{12}$$

$$+ 3\frac{3}{4} \longrightarrow \frac{3}{4} \times \frac{3}{3} \longrightarrow \frac{9}{12}$$

$$5 \qquad\qquad \frac{13}{12}$$

$$5 + 1\frac{1}{12} = 6\frac{1}{12}$$

Add. Simplify if possible.

1. $1\frac{3}{8}$
    $+ 4\frac{1}{6}$

2. $2\frac{3}{4}$
    $+ 3\frac{1}{5}$

3. $5\frac{1}{3}$
    $+ 1\frac{5}{6}$

4. $6\frac{1}{2}$
    $+ \frac{3}{4}$

5. $5\frac{2}{5}$
    $+ 2\frac{1}{3}$

6. $4\frac{1}{6}$
    $+ 2\frac{3}{4}$

7. $4\frac{5}{12}$
    $+ 2\frac{5}{6}$

8. $1\frac{2}{5}$
    $+ 3\frac{7}{10}$

9. $2\frac{3}{8}$
    $+ 7\frac{1}{2}$

Subtracting Fractions with Like Denominators

To subtract fractions with like denominators:

1. Subtract the numerators.
2. Keep the same denominator.
3. Simplify if possible.

$$\begin{array}{r} \frac{7}{8} \\ - \frac{3}{8} \\ \hline \frac{4}{8} = \frac{1}{2} \end{array}$$

Subtract. Simplify if possible.

1. $\begin{array}{r} \frac{3}{8} \\ - \frac{1}{8} \\ \hline \end{array}$

2. $\begin{array}{r} \frac{7}{12} \\ - \frac{5}{12} \\ \hline \end{array}$

3. $\begin{array}{r} \frac{5}{6} \\ - \frac{1}{6} \\ \hline \end{array}$

4. $\begin{array}{r} \frac{11}{12} \\ - \frac{1}{12} \\ \hline \end{array}$

5. $\begin{array}{r} \frac{9}{10} \\ - \frac{3}{10} \\ \hline \end{array}$

6. $\begin{array}{r} \frac{4}{5} \\ - \frac{2}{5} \\ \hline \end{array}$

7. $\begin{array}{r} \frac{3}{4} \\ - \frac{1}{4} \\ \hline \end{array}$

8. $\begin{array}{r} \frac{11}{12} \\ - \frac{5}{12} \\ \hline \end{array}$

9. $\begin{array}{r} \frac{10}{11} \\ - \frac{3}{11} \\ \hline \end{array}$

Subtracting Fractions from a Whole Number

To subtract a fraction from a whole number:

1. Rewrite the whole number as a mixed number with an equivalent fraction using the LCD.
2. Subtract.

$$3 - \frac{1}{4} =$$

$$3 \longrightarrow 2\frac{4}{4}$$

$$-\frac{1}{4} \longrightarrow \frac{1}{4}$$

$$= 2\frac{3}{4}$$

Subtract. Simplify if possible.

1. $5 - \frac{7}{8} =$

2. $3 - \frac{1}{3} =$

3. $6 - \frac{7}{9} =$

4. $8 - \frac{4}{5} =$

5. $5 - \frac{4}{9} =$

6. $12 - \frac{3}{11} =$

7. $7 - \frac{1}{3} =$

8. $10 - \frac{1}{5} =$

9. $12 - \frac{7}{10} =$

Subtracting Mixed Numbers

Rewrite $3\frac{1}{4}$ so you can subtract.

$$3\frac{1}{4} = 2 + 1\frac{1}{4} = 2\frac{5}{4}$$

$$-1\frac{3}{4} \longrightarrow 1\frac{3}{4}$$

$$1\frac{2}{4} = 1\frac{1}{2}$$

Rewrite $6\frac{2}{9}$ so you can subtract.

$$6\frac{2}{9} = 5 + 1\frac{2}{9} = 5\frac{11}{9}$$

$$-5\frac{4}{9} \longrightarrow 5\frac{4}{9}$$

$$\frac{7}{9}$$

Subtract. Simplify if possible.

1. $3\frac{3}{7}$
   $-1\frac{5}{7}$

2. $5\frac{1}{3}$
   $-2\frac{2}{3}$

3. $4\frac{1}{6}$
   $-3\frac{5}{6}$

4. $6\frac{1}{5}$
   $-3\frac{3}{5}$

5. $4\frac{3}{10}$
   $-3\frac{7}{10}$

6. $8\frac{2}{5}$
   $-5\frac{4}{5}$

7. $3\frac{1}{8}$
   $-2\frac{5}{8}$

8. $6\frac{4}{9}$
   $-5\frac{7}{9}$

9. $12\frac{5}{12}$
   $-10\frac{7}{12}$

Subtracting Fractions with Unlike Denominators

To subtract fractions with unlike denominators:

1. Find the LCD.
2. Rewrite using LCD.
3. Subtract.

$$\frac{2}{5} \longrightarrow \frac{2}{5} \times \frac{3}{3} \longrightarrow \frac{6}{15}$$
$$-\frac{1}{3} \longrightarrow \frac{1}{3} \times \frac{5}{5} \longrightarrow \frac{5}{15}$$
$$\frac{1}{15}$$

Subtract. Simplify if possible.

1. $\frac{2}{3}$
   $-\frac{1}{4}$

2. $\frac{4}{5}$
   $-\frac{1}{2}$

3. $\frac{1}{2}$
   $-\frac{1}{3}$

4. $\frac{1}{2}$
   $-\frac{2}{9}$

5. $\frac{2}{3}$
   $-\frac{2}{7}$

6. $\frac{3}{4}$
   $-\frac{1}{5}$

7. $\frac{3}{5}$
   $-\frac{2}{9}$

8. $\frac{7}{8}$
   $-\frac{2}{5}$

9. $\frac{5}{6}$
   $-\frac{1}{7}$

Subtracting Mixed Numbers with Unlike Denominators

Steps for subtracting mixed numbers:

1. Find the LCD.
2. Rewrite the fraction(s) using the LCD.
3. Rewrite again, if needed, to subtract.
4. Subtract.
5. Simplify if possible.

$$8\frac{1}{3} \longrightarrow 8\frac{8}{24} \longrightarrow 7\frac{32}{24}$$
$$-6\frac{5}{8} \longrightarrow 6\frac{15}{24} \longrightarrow 6\frac{15}{24}$$
$$\overline{\phantom{-6\frac{5}{8} \longrightarrow 6\frac{15}{24} \longrightarrow} 1\frac{17}{24}}$$

Subtract. Simplify if possible.

1. $4\frac{1}{3}$
   $-2\frac{1}{2}$

2. $6\frac{1}{8}$
   $-5\frac{1}{6}$

3. $5\frac{1}{4}$
   $-3\frac{1}{2}$

4. $6\frac{3}{8}$
   $-5\frac{3}{4}$

5. $4\frac{2}{9}$
   $-3\frac{2}{3}$

6. $9\frac{1}{6}$
   $-7\frac{1}{3}$

7. $6\frac{1}{3}$
   $-4\frac{5}{8}$

8. $7\frac{1}{4}$
   $-3\frac{7}{8}$

9. $9\frac{3}{10}$
   $-5\frac{4}{5}$

Adding and Subtracting Fractions Review

To add or subtract fractions when the denominators are the same. Add or subtract the numerators. The denominators do not change. Try to picture each problem in your head.

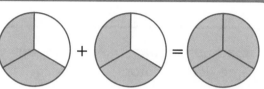

$$\frac{2}{3} + \frac{2}{3} = \frac{4}{3}$$

or $1\frac{1}{3}$

Add or subtract. Rewrite improper fractions as mixed numbers.

1. $\dfrac{2}{6}$
    $-\ \dfrac{1}{6}$

2. $\dfrac{3}{4}$
    $+\ \dfrac{1}{4}$

3. $\dfrac{6}{8}$
    $-\ \dfrac{5}{8}$

4. $\dfrac{4}{5}$
    $+\ \dfrac{1}{5}$

5. $\dfrac{7}{8}$
    $+\ \dfrac{4}{8}$

6. $\dfrac{9}{11}$
    $+\ \dfrac{2}{11}$

7. $\dfrac{3}{10}$
    $+\ \dfrac{3}{10}$

8. $\dfrac{4}{9}$
    $+\ \dfrac{6}{9}$

9. $\dfrac{8}{12}$
    $-\ \dfrac{2}{12}$

Adding and Subtracting Mixed Numbers with Like Denominators

To add or subtract mixed numbers whose fractions have the same denominator:

Step 1
Add or subtract the numerators of the fraction part.

$$2\frac{7}{9}$$
$$+ \ 4\frac{8}{9}$$
$$\overline{\quad \frac{15}{9}}$$

Step 2
Add or subtract the whole numbers.

$$2\frac{7}{9}$$
$$+ \ 4\frac{8}{9}$$
$$\overline{6\frac{15}{9}}$$

Step 3
Simplify.

$$2\frac{7}{9}$$
$$+ \ 4\frac{8}{9}$$
$$\overline{6\frac{15}{9} = 7\frac{6}{9}}$$
$$= 7\frac{2}{3}$$

Write each sum or difference in simplest form.

1. $3\frac{1}{3}$
    $+ \ 1\frac{2}{3}$

2. $6\frac{7}{10}$
    $- \ 2\frac{3}{10}$

3. $4\frac{5}{6}$
    $- \ \frac{1}{6}$

4. $4\frac{1}{2}$
    $+ \ 4\frac{1}{2}$

5. $5\frac{2}{3}$
    $- \ 4$

6. $3\frac{1}{2}$
    $- \ 1\frac{1}{2}$

7. $7\frac{3}{8}$
    $- \ 5$

8. $6\frac{3}{4}$
    $+ \ \frac{3}{4}$

9. $5\frac{11}{14}$
    $- \ 2\frac{3}{14}$

Adding and Subtracting Fractions with Unlike Denominators

Write equivalent fractions with the lowest common denominator. Then add or subtract the numerator. Simplify your answer.

$$\frac{5}{6} = \frac{10}{12}$$
$$+\ \frac{3}{4} = +\ \frac{9}{12}$$
$$\overline{\frac{19}{12} = 1\frac{7}{12}}$$

Add or subtract. Write the answer in simplest form.

1. $\frac{2}{3}$
   $+\ \frac{1}{4}$

2. $\frac{5}{6}$
   $-\ \frac{4}{9}$

3. $\frac{2}{5}$
   $+\ \frac{7}{10}$

4. $\frac{3}{8}$
   $+\ \frac{5}{6}$

5. $\frac{1}{2}$
   $+\ \frac{7}{8}$

6. $\frac{2}{3}$
   $-\ \frac{3}{5}$

7. $\frac{1}{2}$
   $-\ \frac{3}{10}$

8. $\frac{1}{2}$
   $+\ \frac{4}{5}$

9. $\frac{3}{10}$
   $-\ \frac{1}{6}$

10. $\frac{1}{6}$
    $-\ \frac{1}{12}$

11. $\frac{2}{15}$
    $+\ \frac{1}{6}$

12. $\frac{5}{7}$
    $-\ \frac{1}{3}$

Adding and Subtracting Mixed Numbers with Unlike Denominators

Step 1	Step 2	Step 3	Step 4
Write equivalent fractions with the lowest common denominator.	Add or subtract the numerators of the fraction part.	Add or subtract the whole numbers.	Simplify.

$$4\frac{5}{6} = 4\frac{15}{18}$$
$$-1\frac{3}{9} = -1\frac{6}{18}$$

$$4\frac{15}{18}$$
$$-1\frac{6}{18}$$
$$\frac{9}{18}$$

$$4\frac{15}{18}$$
$$-1\frac{6}{18}$$
$$3\frac{9}{18}$$

$$4\frac{15}{18}$$
$$-1\frac{6}{18}$$
$$3\frac{9}{18}$$
$$= 3\frac{1}{2}$$

Add or subtract. Write the answer in simplest form.

1. $4\frac{1}{10}$
   $+ 3\frac{1}{2}$

2. $7\frac{5}{4}$
   $+ 5\frac{1}{6}$

3. $6\frac{7}{8}$
   $+ 2\frac{3}{4}$

4. $12\frac{7}{8}$
   $- 6\frac{1}{3}$

5. $36\frac{1}{2}$
   $- 25\frac{3}{10}$

6. $15\frac{5}{9}$
   $- 9\frac{1}{3}$

7. $12\frac{7}{8}$
   $+ 6\frac{1}{3}$

8. $9\frac{7}{8}$
   $+ 4\frac{5}{6}$

9. $8\frac{1}{10}$
   $+ 5\frac{1}{4}$

Problem Solving

Solve each problem. Write answers in simplest terms.

1. An extra-large pepperoni pizza was cut into 16 equal slices. A total of 10 slices of pizza were eaten. What fraction of the pizza was left over?

2. Four friends shared a pizza. Maria ate $\frac{1}{3}$ of the pizza, Ana and Mandy each ate $\frac{1}{4}$ of the pizza, and Beth ate $\frac{1}{6}$.

   a. Into how many equal slices did they need to cut the pizza?

   b. How many slices of pizza did each girl eat?

3. In a survey on vegetable toppings, $\frac{3}{4}$ of the sixth-grade students said they liked green peppers on their pizza, $\frac{5}{8}$ said they liked mushrooms, and $\frac{2}{3}$ of the students said they liked onions. (Some students liked more than one choice.)

   a. Which of the three choices do more of the students like?

   b. Which of the three choices do the least number of students like?

4. Each medium pizza weighs 54 ounces. The pizza dough alone weighs 21 ounces. What fraction of the pizza's weight is the pizza dough?

Problem Solving:
Fractions in a Bar Graph

The Chamber of Commerce surveyed 36 tourists to see what activities they participated in while visiting the capital city. The graph shows the number of tourists who took part in each activity. Example: 6 of the 36 tourists, or $\frac{6}{36}$, visited museums.

Solve using the graph. Write all fractions in simplest form.

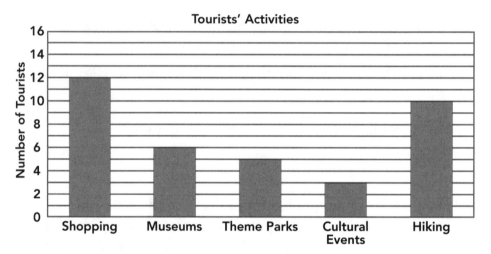

1. Which activity was chosen by $\frac{1}{6}$ of the tourists?

2. What fraction of the tourists participated in the least popular activity?

3. What fraction of the tourists participated in the most popular activity?

4. Which activity did $\frac{5}{36}$ of the tourists participate in?

5. What fraction of the tourists chose hiking?

Problem Solving

Leave answers as fractions. Simplify if possible.

Jobs	Trisha's Time per Task	Tyrone's Time per Task
Homework	$2\frac{1}{4}$ hours	$1\frac{2}{3}$ hours
Clean bathroom	$\frac{3}{4}$ hour	$\frac{1}{2}$ hour
Clean bedroom	$\frac{1}{3}$ hour	1 hour
Walk dog	$\frac{1}{2}$ hour	$\frac{3}{4}$ hour

1. How much total time does it take Trisha and Tyrone to do their homework?

2. How much more time does Trisha spend on her homework than Tyrone?

3. How much more time does Tyrone spend cleaning his bedroom than Trisha?

4. If Tyrone comes home from school, does his homework, and then walks the dog, how much time will it take him?

5. If Trisha cleans only once a week, how much time does she spend cleaning the bathroom and bedroom per week?

6. If Tyrone cleans the bathroom two times a week, and Trisha cleans the bathroom only once a week, who spends more time cleaning the bathroom?

Addition and Subtraction Practice with Magic Squares

When you add the numbers in each row, column, and diagonal of a magic square, the sums are the same. Find the missing numbers in each magic square below. The magic sums are given.

$\frac{4}{15}$		$\frac{8}{15}$
	$\frac{1}{3}$	
$\frac{2}{15}$		$\frac{2}{5}$

The magic sum is 1.

$1\frac{4}{5}$		$2\frac{3}{5}$
	$1\frac{1}{2}$	
	$2\frac{9}{10}$	$1\frac{1}{5}$

The magic sum is $4\frac{1}{2}$.

$1\frac{1}{8}$		$1\frac{3}{8}$
$1\frac{1}{4}$		$1\frac{1}{2}$

The magic sum is $3\frac{15}{16}$.

$2\frac{1}{3}$		$2\frac{4}{9}$
$2\frac{1}{9}$		$2\frac{2}{9}$

The magic sum is $6\frac{5}{6}$.

Probability

Probability is the chance of an event occurring. The probability of an event can be described as **likely**, **unlikely**, **certain**, or **impossible**.

Suppose we fill up a sack with 10 marbles. One is green and 9 are red.

The probability of pulling out a green marble is **unlikely**.

The probability of pulling out a red marble is **likely**.

The probability of pulling out a yellow marble is **impossible**.

The probability of pulling out a green *or* red marble is **certain**.

Look at the spinner to answer the following questions. Write if the probability is likely, unlikely, certain, or impossible.

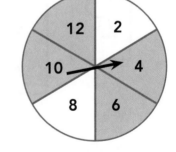

1. The probability of spinning an even number is

   _____.

2. The probability of spinning an odd number is

   _____.

3. The probability of landing on a shaded space is

   _____.

4. The probability of landing on a number greater than 8 is

   _____.

5. The probability of landing on a 2 is

   _____.

Probability

Probability can be written as a fraction.

Look at the spinner to the right.

The probability of landing on a striped space is $\frac{2}{8}$ or $\frac{1}{4}$.

The probability of landing on an even number is $\frac{4}{8}$ or $\frac{1}{2}$.

The probability of landing on 12 is $\frac{0}{8}$ or 0.

The probability of landing on a number less than 10 is $\frac{8}{8}$ or 1.

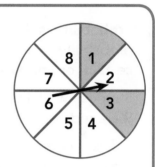

Imagine if we turned over the cards below, mixed them up, and then picked one card. Answer the following questions by writing a fraction.

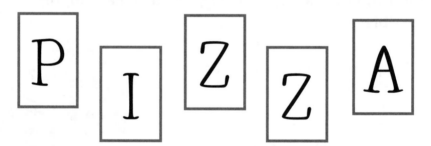

1. What is the probability of picking a P?

2. What is the probability of picking a Z?

3. What is the probability of picking an E?

4. What is the probability of picking a number?

5. What is the probability of picking any letter?

6. What is the probability of picking a vowel?

Probability

Marisa's mother keeps a box full of mismatched socks. In the box there are 5 white, 4 blue, 1 red, 1 gray, and 3 black socks.

What is the probability of pulling out a blue sock?

The probability would equal the number of blue socks over the total number of socks.

$$\frac{\text{Blue}}{\text{Total}} = \frac{4}{5 + 4 + 1 + 1 + 3} = \frac{4}{14} = \frac{2}{7}$$

Holly bought a box of candy that had the following colors inside: 14 brown, 8 yellow, 2 blue, and 6 red. Without looking she pulled out one candy.

1. What is the probability that it is yellow?
2. What is the probability that it is red?
3. What is the probability that it is purple?
4. What is the probability that it is brown?

Ryan sees a fruit basket on the kitchen table. It contains 4 green apples, 5 red apples, and 6 oranges. He grabs one piece of fruit.

5. What is the probability that it is red?
6. What is the probability that it is a fruit?
7. What is the probability that it is an orange?
8. What is the probability that it is an apple?

Probability and Statistics Review

Probability is the chance or possibility that an event will happen.

- If the fraction that describes the probability is equal to 1, the event is certain.
- If the fraction is greater than another, the event is more likely.
- If the fraction is less than another, the event is less likely.
- If the fraction that describes the probability is 0, the event is impossible.

Find the probability. Write it as a fraction.

Penny has 11 pencils in her pencil box. Two pencils are orange, 3 pencils are blue, 5 pencils are yellow, and 1 pencil is green.

1. What is the probability that Penny will pull out an **orange** pencil?

2. What is the probability that Penny will pull out a **green** pencil?

3. What is the probability that Penny will pull out a **blue** pencil?

4. What is the probability that Penny will pull out a **black** pencil?

5. What is the probability that Penny will pull out a **yellow** pencil?

6. What color pencil is Penny **most likely** to pull out of her pencil box?

Multiplying Fractions

$\frac{1}{2} \times \frac{1}{4}$ can be visualized as:

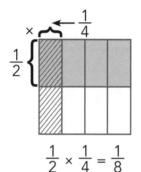

$$\frac{1}{2} \times \frac{1}{4} = \frac{1}{8}$$

The shaded rectangles on the top represent $\frac{1}{2}$ of the entire shape. The patterned rectangles on the left represent $\frac{1}{4}$ of the entire shape. The intersection of these represents $\frac{1}{2} \times \frac{1}{4}$, or $\frac{1}{8}$ of the entire shape.

Use the grids to multiply fractions.

1.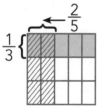

$\frac{1}{3} \times \frac{2}{5}$ _____

2.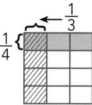

$\frac{1}{4} \times \frac{1}{3}$ _____

3.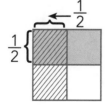

$\frac{1}{2} \times \frac{1}{2}$ _____

4.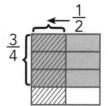

$\frac{3}{4} \times \frac{1}{2}$ _____

Multiplying Fractions

Multiply. Simplify if possible.

1. $\frac{1}{2} \times 1\frac{1}{8}$

2. $\frac{1}{10} \times \frac{1}{3}$

3. $\frac{4}{5} \times \frac{1}{3}$

4. $\frac{5}{8} \times \frac{1}{4}$

5. $\frac{3}{5} \times 3\frac{1}{2}$

6. $\frac{2}{5} \times \frac{1}{7}$

7. $4\frac{3}{4} \times \frac{1}{3}$

8. $\frac{1}{9} \times 2\frac{1}{2}$

9. $\frac{1}{2} \times \frac{1}{2}$

10. $2\frac{2}{3} \times \frac{3}{4}$

11. $9\frac{1}{2} \times \frac{1}{6}$

12. $3\frac{3}{4} \times \frac{5}{12}$

Multiplying Fractions by Whole Numbers

When multiplying a whole number and a fraction:

$$\frac{3}{4} \times 6$$

1. Rewrite the whole number as a fraction (write a denominator of 1).

$$\frac{3}{4} \times \frac{6}{1}$$

2. Multiply the numerators.

$$\frac{18}{4}$$

3. Multiply the denominators.

4. Simplify if possible.

$$4\frac{2}{4} = 4\frac{1}{2}$$

Multiply. Simplify if possible.

1. $3 \times \frac{2}{3}$

2. $\frac{4}{5} \times 2$

3. $1 \times \frac{6}{7}$

4. $\frac{2}{5} \times 6$

5. $3 \times \frac{3}{10}$

6. $9 \times \frac{3}{4}$

7. $8 \times \frac{1}{6}$

8. $2 \times \frac{6}{7}$

9. $6 \times \frac{1}{10}$

10. $\frac{3}{10} \times 5$

11. $5 \times \frac{2}{9}$

12. $\frac{3}{7} \times 2$

Dividing Fractions

To find $\frac{4}{5} \div \frac{3}{4}$, multiply $\frac{4}{5}$ by the reciprocal of $\frac{3}{4}$.

Rewrite $\frac{4}{5} \div \frac{3}{4}$ as $\frac{4}{5} \times \frac{4}{3}$.

Then multiply and simplify: $\frac{4 \times 4}{5 \times 3} = \frac{16}{15} = 1\frac{1}{15}$

So $\frac{4}{5} \div \frac{3}{4} = 1\frac{1}{15}$

Divide. Write each quotient in simplest form.

1. $\frac{5}{6} \div \frac{5}{9}$

2. $\frac{3}{8} \div \frac{3}{4}$

3. $\frac{3}{4} \div \frac{5}{2}$

4. $\frac{5}{8} \div \frac{1}{8}$

5. $\frac{4}{7} \div \frac{2}{7}$

6. $\frac{5}{8} \div \frac{3}{4}$

7. $\frac{5}{4} \div \frac{1}{2}$

8. $\frac{7}{8} \div \frac{3}{5}$

9. $\frac{7}{9} \div \frac{2}{3}$

10. $\frac{11}{6} \div \frac{5}{2}$

11. $\frac{3}{14} \div \frac{6}{7}$

12. $\frac{7}{6} \div \frac{7}{8}$

Problem Solving

Solve each problem. Write each answer in simplest form.

1. Ashton is going to the movie theater. It is $\frac{3}{5}$ of a mile from his house. Ashton decides to take his electric scooter, but it breaks down $\frac{2}{3}$ of the way to the theater. How far is Austin from his house?

   _____

2. Ashton's electric scooter uses $\frac{1}{4}$ gallon of fuel for each mile. How much fuel has he used since he left home?
   (Hint: Use your answer from question 1.)

   _____

3. Ashton purchases $\frac{2}{3}$ pound of Yum-Yum Treats. If Yum-Yum Treats are $6.00 per pound, how much does Ashton pay?

   _____

4. In the theater, Ashton meets 2 of his friends, who have bought 1 gigantic barrel of popcorn. Only $\frac{3}{4}$ of it is left. Ashton eats $\frac{1}{3}$ of what is left. How much of the barrel does Ashton eat?

   _____

Problem Solving

Solve each problem. Write each answer in simplest form.

1. Javon's class has 24 students. If $\frac{1}{8}$ of them play the piano, how many students in his class play the piano?

   _____

2. There are 12 students working in the library. If $\frac{3}{4}$ of them are girls, how many girls are working in the library?

   _____

3. Six students are working on math. Two-thirds of them are working on fractions. How many students are working on fractions?

   _____

4. Javon spent one-fourth of his $\frac{3}{4}$ hour gym class jumping rope. How long did he spend jumping rope?

   _____

Decimals

There are names for place values after the decimal place for numbers smaller than 1.

thousands	hundreds	tens	ones		tenths	hundredths	thousandths
1	2	4	5	.	1	7	6

Study the following.

Decimal	Read As	Equivalent Fraction
0.7	seven-tenths	$\frac{7}{10}$
0.23	twenty-three hundredths	$\frac{23}{100}$
0.05	five-hundredths	$\frac{5}{100}$
0.783	seven hundred eighty-three thousandths	$\frac{783}{1000}$
0.045	forty-five thousandths	$\frac{45}{1000}$
2.6	two and six-tenths	$2\frac{6}{10}$

Complete.

1. 0.3   three-tenths   _____

2. 1.12   _____   _____

3. _____   two hundred twenty-one thousandths   _____

4. _____   _____ $\frac{53}{100}$

5. 0.871   _____   _____

Visualizing Decimals

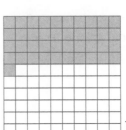

$\frac{5}{10}$ or 0.5

$\frac{41}{100}$ or 0.41

Complete the following.

	Fraction	Decimal
1.	_____	_____
2.	_____	_____
3.	_____	_____
4.	_____	_____

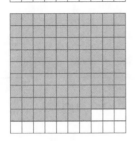

5. _____ _____

6. _____ _____

Converting Decimals into Fractions

Step 1 Move the decimal 2 places to the right.		Step 2 Place the number over 100.	Step 3 Simplify.
0.40	40	$\frac{40}{100}$	$\frac{2}{5}$
1.25	125	$\frac{125}{100}$	$1\frac{1}{4}$
0.5	50	$\frac{50}{100}$	$\frac{1}{2}$

Convert the following decimals into fractions.

1. 0.25

2. 0.02

3. 1.20

4. 0.40

5. 0.15

6. 0.58

7. 5.10

8. 0.80

Converting Fractions into Percentages

Step 1	Step 2
Divide the denominator into the numerator.	Move the decimal 2 places to the right, and add the percent sign (%).

$$\frac{1}{5} = 5\overline{)1.0} \quad \overset{0.2}{}$$

0.20%

Convert the following fractions into percents.

1. $\frac{1}{10}$

2. $\frac{1}{5}$

3. $\frac{4}{5}$

4. $\frac{1}{4}$

5. $\frac{2}{4}$

6. $\frac{1}{10}$

7. $\frac{2}{5}$

8. $\frac{9}{20}$

9. $\frac{3}{4}$

10. $\frac{1}{2}$

Converting Fractions into Decimals

<table>
<tr><td>Step 1
Divide the denominator into the numerator. Add zeros if necessary.

$\frac{1}{3} = 3\overline{)1.000}$</td><td>Step 2
Round to the nearest hundredth.

$\begin{array}{r} 0.333 \\ 3\overline{)1.000} \\ -9 \\ \hline 10 \\ -9 \\ \hline 1 \end{array}$ (etc.)

Round 0.333 to 0.33.</td></tr>
</table>

Convert each fraction into a decimal.

1. $\frac{3}{4}$

2. $\frac{7}{12}$

3. $\frac{1}{10}$

4. $\frac{2}{5}$

5. $\frac{3}{2}$

6. $\frac{1}{6}$

7. $\frac{2}{3}$

8. $\frac{1}{4}$

9. $\frac{5}{4}$

10. $\frac{4}{5}$

11. $\frac{1}{5}$

12. $\frac{3}{8}$

13. $\frac{7}{10}$

14. $\frac{50}{100}$

15. $\frac{1}{2}$

16. $\frac{4}{7}$

Converting Percentages into Fractions

Step 1	Step 2
Put the percent over 100.	Simplify.
20% $\frac{20}{100}$	$\frac{1}{5}$

Convert the following percents into fractions.

1. 5%

2. 23%

3. 10%

4. 50%

5. 75%

6. 2%

7. 40%

8. 100%

Converting Percentages into Decimals

Move a decimal 2 places to the left
and remove the percent sign (%).   **50% = 0.50**

Convert the following percents into decimals.

1. 90% =

2. 40% =

3. 5.1% =

4. 10% =

5. 75% =

6. 25% =

7. 54.6% =

8. 6% =

9. 15% =

10. 48.9% =

11. 8% =

12. 23% =

13. 18% =

14. 51.5% =

15. 9% =

16. 99% =

17. 5.4% =

18. 100% =

Circle Graphs

Favorite Winter Olympic Events

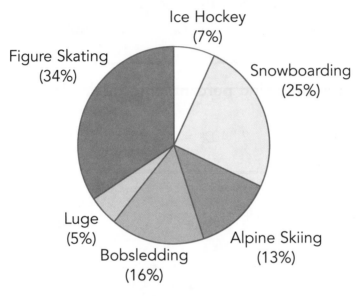

Megan's class voted on their favorite Winter Olympic events. Use the circle graph to answer the questions.

1. Which event received the highest percent of votes?

2. What percent of students voted for bobsledding?

3. Which event did 34% of the students vote for as their favorite?

4. What was the total percentage of students who liked the luge and bobsledding altogether?

5. How many more students voted for snowboarding than alpine skiing?

Fractions, Decimals, and Percents

Write the decimal for each fraction.

$\frac{5}{100}$ = **0.05**   1. $\frac{7}{1000}$ = _____   2. $\frac{92}{100}$ = _____

3. $\frac{84}{1000}$ = _____   4. $\frac{7}{100}$ = _____   5. $\frac{43}{1000}$ = _____

6. $\frac{7}{10}$ = _____   7. $\frac{15}{100}$ = _____   8. $\frac{9}{10}$ = _____

Write the fraction for each decimal.

9. 0.075 = _____   10. 0.03 = _____   11. 0.086 = _____

12. 0.021 = _____   13. 0.04 = _____   14. 0.21 = _____

15. 0.09 = _____   16. 0.11 = _____   17. 0.005 = _____

Write the percent for each decimal.

18. 0.08 = _____   19. 0.19 = _____   20. 0.21 = _____

21. 0.72 = _____   22. 0.33 = _____   23. 0.98 = _____

24. 0.62 = _____   25. 0.07 = _____   26. 0.04 = _____

Missing Numbers:
Fractions, Decimals, and Percents

Write the missing fractions, decimals, and percents in the chart below.

	Fraction	Decimal	Percent
1.	$\frac{5}{100}$	0.05	5%
2.			14%
3.	$\frac{27}{100}$		
4.			32%
5.		0.89	
6.			57%
7.	$\frac{9}{100}$		

Write the letter of the correct point next to its value.

8. 25%

9. $3\frac{1}{2}$

10. 0.75

11. 2.50

12. $\frac{15}{10}$

13. 2.05

Writing Decimal Numbers

Write the missing numbers for the decimal values in the chart below.

	ones	tenths	hundredths	thousandths
1. four-hundredths	0	0	4	
2. six-thousandths				
3. thirty-six thousandths				
4. ten-hundredths				
5. twenty-seven thousandths				
6. ninety-two hundredths				
7. forty-seven thousandths				
8. eighty-nine hundredths				
9. two-tenths				
10. eight-hundredths				

Writing Decimal Numbers

Write the decimal number for each problem.

1. 3 and 6 tenths

2. 1 and 8 hundredths

3. 7 and 2 tenths

4. 4 and 2 thousandths

5. 6 and 1 hundredth

6. 8 and 2 hundredths

7. 3 and 32 thousandths

8. 9 and 7 tenths

Write the decimal number.

9. $108 \frac{7}{10}$ = ____

10. $34 \frac{4}{100}$ = ____

11. $56 \frac{93}{100}$ = ____

12. $20 \frac{9}{100}$ = ____

13. $64 \frac{2}{100}$ = ____

14. $216 \frac{3}{10}$ = ____

15. $81 \frac{5}{10}$ = ____

16. $42 \frac{9}{1000}$ = ___

17. $82 \frac{5}{100}$ = ____

18. $16 \frac{7}{10}$ = ____

19. $38 \frac{5}{10}$ = ____

20. $11 \frac{27}{100}$ = ____

Rounding Decimal Numbers

Find the place value you want to round and look at the digit just to the right of it. If that digit is less than 5, do not change the digit you are rounding. Example: 3.51 is rounded to **3.5**.

If that digit is greater than or equal to 5, add 1 to the digit you are rounding. Example: 3.557 is rounded to **3.56**.

Round each number to the nearest tenth.

1. 2.07 _____

2. 5.67 _____

3. 7.38 _____

4. 5.42 _____

5. 33.01 _____

6. 8.61 _____

7. 7.39 _____

8. 68.96 _____

9. 4.97 _____

10. 26.55 _____

11. 122.18 _____

12. 80.83 _____

Round each number to the nearest hundredth.

13. 3.047 _____

14. 9.921 _____

15. 8.043 _____

16. 62.686 _____

17. 4.769 _____

18. 27.977 _____

19. 1.588 _____

20. 5.815 _____

21. 3.251 _____

22. 51.971 _____

23. 81.745 _____

24. 6.378 _____

Rounding Decimal Numbers

Round each number to the nearest tenth.

1. 4.58

2. 19.96

3. 8.16

4. 12.87

5. 20.08

6. 9.42

Round each number to the nearest hundredth.

7. 6.877

8. 4.058

9. 97.470

10. 8.876

11. 87.069

12. 1.387

Round each number to the nearest thousandth.

13. 1.0649

14. 93.0129

15. 7.2199

16. 22.5240

17. 51.8490

18. 3.7672

Comparing Decimals

Comparing decimals is similar to comparing whole numbers.

Example: 0.08 $\bigcirc$ 0.8

1. Line up the numbers by place value.

    0.08
    0.8

2. Compare the digits left to right. After the decimal point, you have a 0 and an 8. The 8 is bigger than 0, so 0.8 is greater than 0.08.

$$0.08 \enspace < \enspace 0.8$$

Compare each pair of numbers. Use >, <, or =.

1. 0.007 $\bigcirc$ 0.07

2. 2.159 $\bigcirc$ 2.259

3. 10.05 $\bigcirc$ 10.005

4. 0.99 $\bigcirc$ 0.009

5. 30.249 $\bigcirc$ 30.429

6. 0.004 $\bigcirc$ 4.00

7. 6.041 $\bigcirc$ 6.401

8. 92.001 $\bigcirc$ 92.001

9. 263.08 $\bigcirc$ 263.81

10. 0.08 $\bigcirc$ 0.8

11. 101.05 $\bigcirc$ 101.005

12. 9.50 $\bigcirc$ 9.05

13. 214.01 $\bigcirc$ 214.001

14. 9.008 $\bigcirc$ 9.08

Comparing Decimals

Put the prices on the menu in order from least to greatest.

$1.25 $2.03 $1.07 $2.51 $1.10 $2.15 $2.21 $1.05

Item:	Price:
Soda	
Milk	
Fries	
Salad	
Cheese Sandwich	
Tuna Sandwich	
Hamburger	
Cheeseburger	

Circle the largest decimal number in each row.

1. 4.05   4.50   4.005   4.15   4.55   4.5

2. 10.57   10.49   10.005   10.057   10.75   10.094

3. 2.5   2.15   2.52   2.005   2.095   2.51

4. 1.8   1.84   1.48   1.847   1.75   1.5

Adding Decimals

When adding decimals, line up the decimal points.

$$3.5 + 1.06 + 0.45 =$$

Add each column.

$$
\begin{array}{r}
\overset{1\ 1}{3.5} \\
1.06 \\
+\ 0.45 \\
\hline
\mathbf{5.01}
\end{array}
$$

Bring the decimal point straight down.

Add the numbers below. Don't forget the decimal point in your answer.

1. 3.63 + 4.8 =

2. $95.02 + $1.15 =

3. 4.83 + 7.8 + 6.9 =

4. 7.30 + 15.81 + 11 =

5.
$$
\begin{array}{r}
37.5 \\
9.26 \\
+\ 0.07 \\
\hline
\end{array}
$$

6.
$$
\begin{array}{r}
4.2 \\
85.37 \\
+\ 11 \\
\hline
\end{array}
$$

7.
$$
\begin{array}{r}
12.7 \\
286 \\
+\ 0.03 \\
\hline
\end{array}
$$

8. $5.74 + $8.70 + $9.60 =

9. $7.30 + $15.81 + $6.40 =

Subtracting Decimals

When subtracting decimals, line up the decimal points. Use zeros as placeholders where needed.

$$
\begin{array}{r} 5.4 \\ -\,0.17 \end{array}
\qquad
\begin{array}{r} 5.40 \\ -\,0.17 \end{array}
\qquad
\begin{array}{r} 5.\overset{3}{\cancel{4}}0 \\ -\,0.17 \\ \hline \mathbf{5.23} \end{array}
$$

Subtract the decimals below.

1. $\begin{array}{r} 2.6 \\ -\,1.8 \\ \hline \end{array}$

2. $\begin{array}{r} 23.1 \\ -\,0.05 \\ \hline \end{array}$

3. $\begin{array}{r} 6.7 \\ -\,1.6 \\ \hline \end{array}$

4. $\begin{array}{r} 82.3 \\ -\,1.54 \\ \hline \end{array}$

5. $5.4 - 2.1 =$

6. $6.58 - 3.2 =$

7. $41 - 2.6 =$

8. $17.8 - 0.56 =$

9. $7.5 - 0.64 =$

10. $13.9 - 1.25 =$

11. $\begin{array}{r} \$10.40 \\ -\,\$2.43 \\ \hline \end{array}$

12. $\begin{array}{r} \$3.77 \\ -\,\$1.20 \\ \hline \end{array}$

13. $\begin{array}{r} \$17.80 \\ -\,\$11.00 \\ \hline \end{array}$

Which Costs More?

Use the price list to solve each problem. Remember to write the decimal point in your answer.

Item:	Price Per Pound:
apples	$0.97
bananas	$0.56
peaches	$0.72
pears	$0.84
plums	$0.65
oranges	$0.33
grapes	$1.09

1. Anna buys 3 pounds of bananas. Maddie buys 5 pounds of apples. Who spends more, Anna or Maddie?

2. James buys 6 pounds of peaches. How much does James spend on peaches?

3. If Sage buys 4 pounds of oranges and 3 pounds of pears, which fruit does she spend the most money on, oranges or pears?

4. Mason buys 9 pounds of grapes. His sister buys 10 pounds of apples. Who spends more, Mason or his sister?

5. Travis buys 7 pounds of pears. Lisa buys 8 pounds of peaches. Who spends more, Travis or Lisa?

6. Jerry buys 5 pounds of oranges and 4 pounds of bananas. What does he spend the most money on, oranges or bananas?

Multiplying Decimals

Step 1	Step 2	Step 3
Multiply.	Count the number of places (from right to left) over to the decimal point on both numbers.	Place the decimal point in the answer by starting at the right and moving the point the number of spaces you counted.

Step 1:
```
  0.41
× 8.9
  369
3280
3649
```

Step 2:
```
0.41
 .9
```
3 places

Step 3:
```
  0.41
× 8.9
  369
3280
3.649
```

Solve each problem.

1.
```
  5.6
×   8
```

2.
```
0.045
×    6
```

3.
```
  6.21
×    7
```

4.
```
$62.60
×     5
```

5.
```
$2.26
×    3
```

6.
```
  31.2
×   48
```

7.
```
0.725
×   54
```

8.
```
  66.1
×  5.7
```

9.
```
  67.2
× 0.28
```

10.
```
0.532
× 0.64
```

11. 0.3 × 4.61 =

12. 0.32 × 0.81 =

13. 2.51 × 40 =

Dividing Decimals

When finding a unit cost, divide the total cost by the number of units:

Total Cost ÷ Number of Units = Unit Cost

Example:

Maria bought a 15-ounce bag of tortilla chips for **$2.25**. What is the cost per ounce?

$$
\begin{array}{r}
0.15 \\
15\overline{)2.25} \\
-15 \\
\hline
75 \\
-75 \\
\hline
0
\end{array}
$$

← Unit Cost (per ounce)

Total Cost

Number of Units →

The bag of chips cost $0.15 per ounce.

Solve each problem.

1. At Orchard Street Market, 4.5 pounds of pears cost $2.97. What is the cost per pound?

2. Mrs. Parks bought 30 ice cream bars for her daughter's class party. She paid $12.60. How much did each ice cream bar cost?

3. Sandy bought a 32.5-ounce package of mixed nuts for $7.15. What was the cost per ounce?

4. A $2.56 can of mix makes 64 cups of lemonade. What is the cost per 8-ounce cup?

5. Whole watermelons are sold for $3.99 each. Sonia bought a watermelon that weighed 21 pounds. What price per pound did she pay?

Dividing Decimals

Solve each problem. Remember to write the decimal point in your answer.

$$
\begin{array}{r}
4.25 \\
6\overline{)25.50} \\
24 \\
\overline{15} \\
-12 \\
\overline{30} \\
-30 \\
\overline{0}
\end{array}
$$

1. $7\overline{)3.99}$

2. $3\overline{)83.7}$

3. $3\overline{)19.05}$

4. $7\overline{)11.62}$

5. $4\overline{)49.12}$

6. $8\overline{)1.96}$

7. $7\overline{)55.86}$

8. $2\overline{)12.62}$

9. $4\overline{)3.04}$

10. $2\overline{)1.826}$

11. $9\overline{)5.526}$

Dividing Decimals

Step 1	Step 2	Additional Step
Move the decimal points to make the divisor a whole number $0.06\overline{)0.084}$	Divide. $\begin{array}{r} 14 \\ 6\overline{)8.4} \\ -6 \\ \hline 24 \\ -24 \\ \hline 0 \end{array}$	Add zeros if needed. $\begin{array}{r} 5 \\ 5\overline{)28} \\ 25 \\ \hline 3 \end{array}$ $\quad$ $\begin{array}{r} 5.6 \\ 5\overline{)28.0} \\ 25 \\ \hline 30 \end{array}$

Solve each problem.

1. $4\overline{)0.166}$ 2. $0.4\overline{).48}$ 3. $0.6\overline{)1.8}$ 4. $5\overline{)0.95}$

5. $7\overline{)7.14}$ 6. $0.6\overline{)0.198}$ 7. $0.9\overline{)42.3}$ 8. $0.6\overline{)48.90}$

9. $4\overline{)3.62}$ 10. $50\overline{)7.25}$ 11. $25\overline{)2.26}$ 12. $0.03\overline{)0.0009}$

Multiplying Decimals

Solve each problem. Remember to write the decimal point in your answer.

$$
\begin{array}{r}
{\scriptstyle 5\ 3} \\
2.64 \\
\times\ \ 9 \\
\hline
\mathbf{23.76}
\end{array}
$$

1.
$$
\begin{array}{r}
6.48 \\
\times\ \ 7 \\
\hline
\end{array}
$$

2.
$$
\begin{array}{r}
72.7 \\
\times\ \ 8 \\
\hline
\end{array}
$$

3.
$$
\begin{array}{r}
12.9 \\
\times\ 17 \\
\hline
\end{array}
$$

4.
$$
\begin{array}{r}
54.87 \\
\times\ \ 24 \\
\hline
\end{array}
$$

5.
$$
\begin{array}{r}
97.02 \\
\times\ \ 32 \\
\hline
\end{array}
$$

6.
$$
\begin{array}{r}
3.348 \\
\times\ \ 63 \\
\hline
\end{array}
$$

7.
$$
\begin{array}{r}
4.05 \\
\times\ 69 \\
\hline
\end{array}
$$

8.
$$
\begin{array}{r}
2.469 \\
\times\ 236 \\
\hline
\end{array}
$$

9.
$$
\begin{array}{r}
6.009 \\
\times\ \ 48 \\
\hline
\end{array}
$$

10.
$$
\begin{array}{r}
71.865 \\
\times\ \ \ 45 \\
\hline
\end{array}
$$

11.
$$
\begin{array}{r}
98.077 \\
\times\ \ \ 45 \\
\hline
\end{array}
$$

Answer Key

Page 3
1. $\frac{5}{6}$ 2. $\frac{1}{8}$ 3. $\frac{2}{3}$
4. $\frac{4}{8}$ 5. $\frac{16}{32}$ 6. $\frac{3}{12}$

Page 4
1. $\frac{3}{8}, \frac{5}{8}; \frac{4}{6}, \frac{2}{6}, \frac{4}{8}, \frac{4}{8};$
2. $\frac{1}{2}, \frac{1}{2}; \frac{2}{3}, \frac{1}{3}; \frac{1}{4}, \frac{3}{4};$
3. $\frac{1}{2}, \frac{1}{2}; \frac{1}{3}, \frac{2}{3}; \frac{2}{3}, \frac{1}{3};$
4. $\frac{3}{6}, \frac{3}{6}; \frac{1}{6}, \frac{5}{6}, \frac{2}{6}, \frac{4}{6};$

Page 5
1.
2.
3.
4.
5.

Page 6
1. $\frac{3}{5}$ 2. $\frac{4}{9}$
3. $\frac{1}{3}$ 4. $\frac{2}{8}$
5. $\frac{4}{5}$ 6. $\frac{1}{2}$
7. one-third
8. one-half
9. three-eighths
10. two-fifths

Page 7
1. > 2. > 3. >
4. > 5. < 6. >
7. < 8. < 9. <
10. < 11. < 12. <

Page 8
1. $\frac{3}{2}, 1\frac{1}{2}$ 2. $\frac{11}{6}, 1\frac{5}{6}$ 3. $\frac{6}{5}, 1\frac{1}{5}$
4. $\frac{7}{3}, 2\frac{1}{3}$ 5. $\frac{11}{4}, 2\frac{3}{4}$ 6. $\frac{17}{6}, 2\frac{5}{6}$

Page 9
1. $1\frac{1}{4}$ 2. $3\frac{1}{3}$ 3. $1\frac{1}{8}$
4. $2\frac{1}{2}$ 5. $1\frac{3}{4}$ 6. 3
7. $1\frac{3}{7}$ 8. $2\frac{3}{8}$ 9. $1\frac{4}{5}$
10. $2\frac{3}{10}$ 11. $2\frac{1}{8}$ 12. $4\frac{1}{3}$
13. $3\frac{1}{9}$ 14. $2\frac{1}{4}$ 15. $2\frac{1}{6}$

Page 10
1. $7\frac{1}{2}$ 2. $1\frac{3}{4}$ 3. $2\frac{6}{7}$
4. $8\frac{3}{5}$ 5. $2\frac{7}{8}$ 6. $4\frac{1}{5}$
7. $2\frac{7}{12}$ 8. $2\frac{1}{2}$ 9. $1\frac{5}{8}$
10. $2\frac{3}{4}$ 11. $5\frac{4}{9}$ 12. $6\frac{5}{6}$

Page 11
1. $\frac{7}{3}$ 2. $\frac{27}{4}$ 3. $\frac{13}{12}$
4. $\frac{25}{8}$ 5. $\frac{38}{5}$ 6. $\frac{19}{10}$
7. $\frac{17}{5}$ 8. $\frac{103}{11}$ 9. $\frac{27}{7}$
10. $\frac{29}{5}$ 11. $\frac{53}{12}$ 12. $\frac{73}{11}$

Page 12
1. $\frac{1}{4}$ 2. $\frac{2}{5}$ 3. $\frac{1}{3}$
4. $\frac{2}{3}$ 5. $\frac{1}{3}$ 6. $\frac{3}{5}$
7. $\frac{3}{4}$ 8. $\frac{1}{12}$ 9. $\frac{2}{3}$
10. $\frac{1}{3}$ 11. $\frac{1}{4}$ 12. $\frac{5}{6}$

Page 13
1. $2\frac{1}{2}$ 2. $3\frac{1}{3}$ 3. $2\frac{3}{4}$
4. $1\frac{2}{3}$ 5. $6\frac{1}{2}$ 6. 7
7. $2\frac{1}{4}$ 8. $4\frac{1}{3}$ 9. $1\frac{1}{2}$
10. $4\frac{1}{3}$ 11. $5\frac{1}{4}$ 12. $2\frac{1}{4}$

Answer Key

Page 14

1. $\frac{1}{3}$
2. $\frac{2}{3}$
3. $\frac{5}{6}$
4. $\frac{3}{4}$
5. $\frac{1}{6}$
6. $\frac{1}{2}$
7. $1\frac{1}{8}$
8. $2\frac{1}{5}$
9. $2\frac{2}{3}$
10. $5\frac{1}{3}$
11. $1\frac{1}{2}$
12. $4\frac{1}{2}$
13. $1\frac{1}{3}$
14. $2\frac{2}{3}$
15. $4\frac{1}{4}$

Page 15

1. 9
2. 12
3. 4
4. 4
5. 15
6. 12
7. 15
8. 4
9. 10

Page 16

1. $\frac{1}{3} = \frac{2}{6}$ $\frac{3}{9}$ $\cancel{\frac{4}{8}}$ $\frac{5}{15}$
2. $\frac{1}{2} = \frac{2}{8}$ $\cancel{\frac{3}{6}}$ $\frac{4}{16}$ $\frac{5}{20}$
3. $\frac{1}{5} = \cancel{\frac{2}{6}}$ $\frac{2}{10}$ $\frac{3}{15}$ $\frac{4}{20}$
4. $\frac{2}{3} = \frac{4}{6}$ $\frac{6}{9}$ $\cancel{\frac{8}{16}}$ $\frac{10}{15}$
5. $\frac{3}{12}$
6. $\frac{2}{3}$
7. $\frac{10}{16}$
8. $\frac{9}{12}$
9. $\frac{1}{6}$
10. $\frac{6}{9}$

Page 17

1. 6: 1, 2, 3, 6
   18: 1, 2, 3, 6, 9, 18
   GCF: 6
2. 4: 1, 2, 4
   12: 1, 2, 3, 4, 6, 12
   GCF: 4
3. 12: 1, 2, 3, 4, 6, 12
   18: 1, 2, 3, 6, 9, 18
   GCF: 6
4. 14: 1, 2, 7, 14
   21: 1, 3, 7, 21
   GCF: 7
5. 18: 1, 2, 3, 6, 9, 18
   27: 1, 3, 9, 27
   GCF: 9
6. 24: 1, 2, 3, 4, 6, 8, 12, 24
   32: 1, 2, 4, 8, 16, 32
   GCF: 8
7. 9: 1, 3, 9
   12: 1, 2, 3, 4, 6, 12
   GCF: 3
8. 9: 1, 3, 9
   15: 1, 3, 5, 15
   GCF: 3

Page 18

1. $\frac{2}{3}$
2. $\frac{1}{2}$
3. $\frac{3}{5}$
4. $\frac{1}{9}$
5. $\frac{5}{18}$
6. $\frac{5}{6}$
7. $\frac{2}{7}$
8. $\frac{2}{3}$
9. $\frac{11}{15}$
10. $\frac{1}{3}$
11. $\frac{1}{2}$
12. $\frac{4}{5}$
13. $\frac{34}{59}$
14. $\frac{1}{4}$
15 $\frac{13}{14}$

Page 19

1. 6: 6, 12, 18, 24
   2: 2, 4, 6, 8, 10
   LCM: 6
2. 4: 4, 8, 12, 16, 20
   8: 8, 16, 24, 32
   LCM: 8
3. 5: 5, 10, 15, 20
   3: 3, 6, 9, 12, 15, 18
   LCM: -15
4. 4: 4, 8, 12, 16
   6: 6, 12, 18, 24
   LCM: 12
5. 8: 8, 16, 24, 32, 40
   12: 12, 24, 36, 48
   LCM: 24
6. 6: 6, 12, 18, 24, 30
   10: 10, 20, 30, 40, 50
   LCM: 30
7. 12: 12, 24, 36, 48, 60
   20: 20, 40, 60, 80
   LCM: 60
8. 10: 10, 20, 30, 40, 50
   15: 15, 30, 45, 60
   LCM: 30
9. 8: 8, 16, 24, 32, 40
   10: 10, 20, 30, 40, 50
   LCM: 40
10. 4: 4, 8, 12, 16, 20, 24, 28, 32, 36
    18: 18, 36, 54, 72
    LCM: 36

Page 20

1. $\frac{1}{9}$, $\frac{3}{9}$
2. $\frac{2}{6}$, $\frac{1}{6}$
3. $\frac{12}{24}$, $\frac{16}{24}$
4. $\frac{6}{18}$, $\frac{6}{18}$
5. $\frac{14}{28}$, $\frac{12}{28}$
6. $\frac{16}{24}$, $\frac{18}{24}$
7. $\frac{2}{16}$, $\frac{1}{16}$
8. $\frac{1}{12}$, $\frac{3}{12}$
9. $\frac{12}{18}$, $\frac{3}{18}$
10. $\frac{8}{32}$, $\frac{4}{32}$

Answer Key

Page 21
1. $=$ 2. $>$ 3. $>$
4. $>$ 5. $<$ 6. $>$
7. $<$ 8. $>$ 9. $=$
10. $\frac{1}{3}$, $\frac{7}{12}$, $\frac{5}{6}$ 11. $\frac{3}{4}$, $\frac{13}{16}$, $\frac{7}{8}$
12. $\frac{1}{2}$, $\frac{3}{4}$, $\frac{5}{6}$ 13. $\frac{3}{8}$, $\frac{3}{7}$, $\frac{3}{5}$

Page 22
1. 2 2. $\frac{1}{4}$ cup
3. $2\frac{1}{2}$ teaspoons 4. $7\frac{1}{2}$ cups
5. $2\frac{1}{2}$ cups 6. coconut

Page 23
1. $\frac{1}{4}$; $\frac{2}{4}$; $\frac{3}{4}$ 2. $\frac{3}{8}$; $\frac{2}{8}$; $\frac{5}{8}$

Page 24
1. $\frac{4}{5}$ 2. $\frac{2}{3}$ 3. $\frac{2}{3}$
4. $\frac{3}{7}$ 5. $\frac{1}{2}$ 6. $\frac{5}{12}$
7. $\frac{5}{6}$ 8. $\frac{4}{11}$ 9. $\frac{3}{4}$
10. $\frac{4}{9}$ 11. $\frac{2}{3}$ 12. $\frac{7}{11}$

Page 25
1. $5\frac{2}{3}$ 2. $4\frac{3}{5}$ 3. 6
4. $6\frac{1}{5}$ 5. $14\frac{1}{2}$ 6. $4\frac{1}{2}$
7. 13 8. $6\frac{1}{3}$ 9. $4\frac{1}{10}$
10. $5\frac{3}{4}$ 11. $8\frac{1}{3}$ 12. $18\frac{1}{3}$

Page 26
1. $\frac{11}{15}$ 2. $\frac{17}{24}$ 3. $\frac{5}{6}$
4. $1\frac{7}{30}$ 5. $\frac{20}{21}$ 6. $\frac{19}{30}$
7. $\frac{25}{28}$ 8. $\frac{23}{24}$ 9. $1\frac{1}{12}$

Page 27
1. $5\frac{13}{24}$ 2. $5\frac{19}{20}$ 3. $7\frac{1}{6}$
4. $7\frac{1}{4}$ 5. $7\frac{11}{15}$ 6. $6\frac{11}{12}$
7. $7\frac{1}{4}$ 8. $5\frac{1}{10}$ 9. $9\frac{7}{8}$

Page 28
1. $\frac{1}{4}$ 2. $\frac{1}{6}$ 3. $\frac{2}{3}$
4. $\frac{5}{6}$ 5. $\frac{3}{5}$ 6. $\frac{2}{5}$
7. $\frac{1}{2}$ 8. $\frac{1}{2}$ 9. $\frac{7}{11}$

Page 29
1. $4\frac{1}{8}$ 2. $2\frac{2}{3}$ 3. $5\frac{2}{9}$
4. $7\frac{1}{5}$ 5. $4\frac{5}{9}$ 6. $11\frac{8}{11}$
7. $6\frac{2}{3}$ 8. $9\frac{4}{5}$ 9. $11\frac{3}{10}$

Page 30
1. $1\frac{5}{7}$ 2. $2\frac{2}{3}$ 3. $\frac{1}{3}$
4. $2\frac{3}{5}$ 5. $\frac{3}{5}$ 6. $2\frac{3}{5}$
7. $\frac{1}{2}$ 8. $\frac{2}{3}$ 9. $1\frac{5}{6}$

Page 31
1. $\frac{5}{12}$ 2. $\frac{3}{10}$ 3. $\frac{1}{6}$
4. $\frac{5}{18}$ 5. $\frac{8}{21}$ 6. $\frac{11}{20}$
7. $\frac{17}{45}$ 8. $\frac{19}{40}$ 9. $\frac{29}{42}$

Page 32
1. $1\frac{5}{6}$ 2. $\frac{23}{24}$ 3. $1\frac{3}{4}$
4. $\frac{5}{8}$ 5. $\frac{5}{9}$ 6. $1\frac{5}{6}$
7. $1\frac{17}{24}$ 8. $3\frac{3}{8}$ 9. $3\frac{1}{2}$

Page 33
1. $\frac{1}{6}$ 2. 1 3. $\frac{1}{8}$
4. 1 5. $1\frac{3}{8}$ 6. 1
7. $\frac{3}{5}$ 8. $1\frac{1}{9}$ 9. $\frac{1}{2}$

Page 34
1. 5 2. $4\frac{2}{5}$ 3. $4\frac{2}{3}$
4. 9 5. $1\frac{2}{3}$ 6. 2
7. $2\frac{3}{8}$ 8. $7\frac{1}{2}$ 9. $3\frac{4}{7}$

Page 35
1. $\frac{11}{12}$ 2. $\frac{7}{18}$ 3. $1\frac{1}{10}$
4. $1\frac{5}{24}$ 5. $1\frac{3}{8}$ 6. $\frac{1}{15}$
7. $\frac{1}{5}$ 8. $1\frac{3}{10}$ 9. $\frac{2}{15}$
10. $\frac{1}{12}$ 11. $\frac{3}{10}$ 12. $\frac{8}{21}$

Page 36
1. $7\frac{3}{5}$ 2. $13\frac{5}{12}$ 3. $9\frac{5}{8}$
4. $6\frac{13}{24}$ 5. $11\frac{1}{5}$ 6. $6\frac{2}{9}$
7. $19\frac{5}{24}$ 8. $14\frac{17}{24}$ 9. $13\frac{7}{20}$

Answer Key

Page 37
1. $\frac{6}{16}$ or $\frac{3}{8}$ of the pizza
2. a. 12 slices
   b. Maria = 4 slices, Ana = 3 slices, Mandy = 3-slices, Beth = 2 slices
3. a. green peppers b. mushrooms
4. $\frac{21}{54}$ or $\frac{7}{18}$

Page 38
1. Museums
2. $\frac{1}{12}$
3. $\frac{1}{3}$
4. Theme parks
5. $\frac{5}{18}$

Page 39
1. $3\frac{11}{12}$ hours
2. $\frac{7}{12}$ hour
3. $\frac{2}{3}$ hour
4. $2\frac{5}{12}$ hours
5. $1\frac{1}{12}$ hours
6. Tyrone

Page 40
1. $\frac{1}{5}$ $\frac{3}{5}$ $\frac{1}{15}$ $\frac{7}{15}$
2. $\frac{1}{10}$ $2\frac{3}{10}$ $\frac{7}{10}$ $\frac{2}{5}$
3. $1\frac{7}{16}$ $1\frac{9}{16}$ $1\frac{5}{16}$ $1\frac{1}{16}$ $1\frac{3}{16}$
4. $2\frac{1}{18}$ $2\frac{7}{18}$ $2\frac{5}{18}$ $2\frac{1}{6}$ $2\frac{1}{2}$

Page 41
1. certain
2. impossible
3. likely
4. unlikely
5. unlikely

Page 42
1. $\frac{1}{5}$
2. $\frac{2}{5}$
3. 0
4. 0
5. 1
6. $\frac{2}{5}$

Page 43
1. $\frac{4}{15}$
2. $\frac{1}{5}$
3. 0
4. $\frac{7}{15}$
5. $\frac{1}{3}$
6. 1
7. $\frac{2}{5}$
8. $\frac{3}{5}$

Page 44
1. $\frac{2}{11}$
2. $\frac{1}{11}$
3. $\frac{3}{11}$
4. 0
5. $\frac{5}{11}$
6. yellow

Page 45
1. $\frac{2}{15}$
2. $\frac{1}{12}$
3. $\frac{1}{4}$
4. $\frac{3}{8}$

Page 46
1. $\frac{9}{16}$
2. $\frac{1}{30}$
3. $\frac{4}{15}$
4. $\frac{5}{32}$
5. $2\frac{1}{10}$
6. $\frac{2}{35}$
7. $1\frac{7}{12}$
8. $\frac{5}{18}$
9. $\frac{1}{4}$
10. 2
11. $1\frac{7}{12}$
12. $1\frac{9}{16}$

Page 47
1. 2
2. $1\frac{3}{5}$
3. $\frac{6}{7}$
4. $2\frac{2}{5}$
5. $\frac{9}{10}$
6. $6\frac{3}{4}$
7. $1\frac{1}{3}$
8. $1\frac{5}{7}$
9. $\frac{3}{5}$
10. $1\frac{1}{2}$
11. $1\frac{1}{9}$
12. $\frac{6}{7}$

Page 48
1. $1\frac{1}{2}$
2. $\frac{1}{2}$
3. $\frac{3}{10}$
4. 5
5. 2
6. $\frac{5}{6}$
7. $2\frac{1}{2}$
8. $1\frac{11}{24}$
9. $1\frac{1}{6}$
10. $\frac{11}{15}$
11. $\frac{1}{4}$
12. $1\frac{1}{3}$

Page 49
1. $\frac{2}{5}$ miles
2. $\frac{1}{10}$ gallon
3. $4.00
4. $\frac{1}{4}$ barrel

Page 50
1. 3 students
2. 9 girls
3. 4 students
4. $\frac{3}{16}$ hour

Page 51
1. $\frac{3}{10}$
2. one and twelve-hundredths; $1\frac{12}{100}$
3. 0.221; $\frac{221}{1000}$
4. 0.53; fifty-three hundredths
5. eight hundred seventy-one thousandths; $\frac{871}{1000}$

Answer Key

Page 52
1. $\frac{2}{10}$; 0.2
2. $\frac{8}{10}$; 0.8
3. $\frac{9}{10}$; 0.9
4. $\frac{1}{10}$; 0.1
5. $\frac{13}{100}$; 0.13
6. $\frac{87}{100}$; 0.87

Page 53
1. $\frac{25}{100}$ or $\frac{1}{4}$
2. $\frac{2}{100}$ or $\frac{1}{50}$
3. $\frac{120}{100}$ or $1\frac{1}{5}$
4. $\frac{40}{100}$ or $\frac{2}{5}$
5. $\frac{15}{100}$ or $\frac{3}{20}$
6. $\frac{58}{100}$ or $\frac{29}{50}$
7. $\frac{510}{100}$ or $5\frac{1}{10}$
8. $\frac{80}{100}$ or $\frac{4}{5}$

Page 54
1. 10%   2. 20%   3. 80%   4. 25%
5. 50%   6. 10%   7. 40%   8. 45%
9. 75% 10. 50%

Page 55
1. 0.75   2. 0.58   3. 0.10
4. 0.40   5. 1.50   6. 0.17
7. 0.67   8. 0.25   9. 1.25
10. 0.80   11. 0.20   12. 0.38
13. 0.70   14. 0.50   15. 0.50
16. 0.57

Page 56
1. $\frac{5}{100}$ or $\frac{1}{20}$
2. $\frac{23}{100}$
3. $\frac{20}{100}$ or $\frac{1}{10}$
4. $\frac{50}{100}$ or $\frac{1}{2}$
5. $\frac{75}{100}$ or $\frac{3}{4}$
6. $\frac{2}{100}$ or $\frac{1}{50}$
7. $\frac{40}{100}$ or $\frac{2}{5}$
8. $\frac{100}{100}$ or 1

Page 57
1. 0.90   2. 0.40   3. 0.051
4. 0.10   5. 0.75   6. 0.25
7. 0.546   8. 0.06   9. 0.15
10. 0.489 11. 0.08   12. 0.23
13. 0.18   14. 0.515   15. 0.09
16. 0.99   17. 0.054   18. 1

Page 58
1. figure skating   2. 16%
3. figure skating   4. 21%
5. 12%

Page 59
1. 0.007   2. 0.92   3. 0.084
4. 0.07   5. 0.043   6. 0.7
7. 0.15   8. 0.9
9. $\frac{75}{100}$ 10. $\frac{3}{100}$ 11. $\frac{86}{1000}$
12. $\frac{21}{1000}$ 13. $\frac{4}{100}$ 14. $\frac{21}{100}$
15. $\frac{9}{100}$ 16. $\frac{11}{100}$ 17. $\frac{5}{1000}$
18. 8%   19. 19%   20. 21%
21. 72%   22. 33%   23. 98%
24. 62%   25. 7%   26. 4%

Page 60
1. $\frac{5}{100}$ 0.05 5%   2. $\frac{14}{100}$ 0.14 14%
3. $\frac{27}{100}$ 0.27 27%   4. $\frac{32}{100}$ 0.32 32%
5. $\frac{89}{100}$ 0.89 89%   6. $\frac{57}{100}$ 0.57 57%
7. $\frac{9}{100}$ 0.09 9   8. B
9. D   10. E
11. A   12. C
13. F

Page 61
1. 0.04   2. 0.006   3. 0.036
4. 0.10   5. 0.027   6. 0.92
7. 0.047   8. 0.89   9. 0.2
10. 0.08

Page 62
1. 3.6   2. 1.08   3. 7.2
4. 4.002   5. 6.01   6. 8.02
7. 3.032   8. 9.7   9. 108.7
10. 34.04   11. 56.93   12. 20.09
13. 64.02   14. 216.3   15. 81.5
16. 42.009   17. 82.05   18. 16.7
19. 38.5   20. 11.27

Answer Key

Page 63
1. 2.1	2. 5.7	3. 7.4
4. 5.4	5. 33.0	6. 8.6
7. 7.4	8. 69.0	9. 5.0
10. 26.6	11. 122.2	12. 80.8
13. 3.05	14. 9.92	15. 8.04
16. 62.69	17. 4.77	18. 27.98
19. 1.59	20. 5.82	21. 3.25
22. 51.97	23. 81.75	24. 6.38

Page 64
1. 4.6	2. 20.0	3. 8.2
4. 12.9	5. 20.1	6. 9.4
7. 6.88	8. 4.06	9. 97.47
10. 8.88	11. 87.07	12. 1.39
13. 1.065	14. 93.013	15. 7.220
16. 22.524	17. 51.849	18. 3.767

Page 65
1. <	2. <	3. >	4. >
5. <	6. <	7. <	8. =
9. <	10. <	11. >	12. >
13. >	14. <		

Page 66
Soda $1.05; Milk $1.07; Fries $1.10; Salad $1.25; Cheese Sandwich $2.03; Tuna Sandwich $2.15; Hamburger $2.21; Cheeseburger $2.51

1. 4.55	2. 10.75
3. 2.52	4. 1.847

Page 67
1. 8.43	2. $96.17	3. 19.53
4. 34.11	5. 46.83	6. 100.57
7. 298.73	8. $24.04	9. $29.51

Page 68
1. 0.8	2. 23.05	3. 5.1
4. 80.76	5. 3.3	6. 3.38
7. 38.4	8. 17.24	9. 6.86
10. 12.65	11. $7.97	12. $2.57
13. $6.80		

Page 69
1. Maddie	2. $4.32	3. pears
4. Mason	5. Travis	6. bananas

Page 70
1. 44.8	2. 0.27	3. 43.47
4. $313	5. $6.78	6. 1,497.6
7. 39.15	8. 376.77	9. 18.816
10. 0.34048	11. 1.383	12. 0.2592
13. 100.4		

Page 71
1. $0.66

2. $0.42

3. $0.22

4. $0.04

5. $0.19

Page 72
1. 0.57	2. 27.9	3. 6.35
4. 1.66	5. 12.28	6. 0.245
7. 7.98	8. 6.31	9. 0.76
10. 0.913	11. 0.614	

Page 73
1. 0.0415	2. 1.2	3. 3
4. 0.19	5. 1.02	6. 0.33
7. 47	8. 81.5	9. 0.905
10. 0.145	11. 0.0904	12. 0.03

Page 74
1. 45.36	2. 581.6
3. 219.3	4. 1,316.88
5. 3,104.64	6. 210.924
7. 279.45	8. 582.684
9. 288.432	10. 3,233.925
11. 4,413.465	